Original title:
Wildflower Writings

Copyright © 2025 Creative Arts Management OÜ
All rights reserved.

Author: Evan Hawthorne
ISBN HARDBACK: 978-1-80566-774-2
ISBN PAPERBACK: 978-1-80566-794-0

Epistles from the Evergreen

Trees gossip in whispers, so sweet,
Their stories of squirrels, with nimble feet.
Pine cones debate on who's the best,
While moss laughs quietly, feeling blessed.

The branches swing low in a comical sway,
As critters hold court at the end of the day.
With laughter from loamy, soft forest beds,
And insects that dance in their light-hearted threads.

Musing of the Meadowlark

A lark sings a tune, quite absurd,
About a lost hat and a silly old bird.
With wiggles and twirls, it leaps on the grass,
In a bizarre ballet where no one can pass.

The daisies giggle, their petals in bloom,
As bees buzz around in a fanciful zoom.
They plot a parade with the ants in the line,
All marching together, feeling just fine.

Starlit Petals

Beneath a sky sprinkled with stars,
Petals have dreams and talk of guitars.
They strum on their stems, in the cool evening breeze,
While fireflies join in, flashing with ease.

"Don't step on me," a bold lily exclaimed,
"As everyone knows, I'm quite well-claimed!"
The moon chuckled softly, hearing their plight,
As flowers debated who'd bloom most bright.

Nature's Unwritten Story

In the woods, if you listen, there's laughter galore,
A tale told by whimsy, an open-air lore.
A rabbit, quite proud, thinks he's a swift knight,
While twigs play conspirators in the moonlight.

The brook babbles merrily, spilling its tea,
As frogs in their hats dance uncouthly with glee.
Nature insists on a comedy spree,
Where every leaf tells a joke, just for free!

Echoes Among the Blossoms

In a field where daisies giggle,
Buttercups dance and then wiggle,
Bees in bow ties buzz quite loud,
While tulips softly join the crowd.

Sunflowers wear their sunny crowns,
Telling tales of laughing clowns,
The breeze whispers silly jokes,
As petals chuckle with the folks.

Stitches of the Soil

The ground's a quilt of colors bright,
With worms that wiggle left and right,
A patch of carrots tells a tale,
Of sneaky rabbits on the trail.

Radishes roll in laughter's glee,
While spinach sings a funny spree,
Tomatoes toss a joke or two,
As broccoli dances, green and true.

Symphony of Prairie Colors

A concert of hues bursts forth in play,
With violets crooning all the way,
The thistle strums its prickly tune,
Underneath the watchful moon.

With daisies clapping, what a sight,
As poppies pirouette in delight,
The wind's a conductor, waving high,
While butterflies flutter, oh my, oh my!

Ramblings of the Roaming Roots

Roots dig deep, with stories bold,
Of adventures beneath the gold,
They chuckle at the timid rains,
And poke fun at the passing trains.

With each twist and curl they share,
Tales of worms with funky hair,
From nutty nuts to loony leaves,
They weave a web of tails and thieves.

A Palette for the Untamed

In fields where poppies dance so free,
They gossip with the bumblebee.
Each petal painted bold and bright,
They hold a party every night.

The daisies debate who's more divine,
While thistles sip garden wine.
Oh, dandelions make a fuss,
Claiming they're the fit for us.

Sunflowers wear hats of gold so grand,
Spinning tales of a sunflower band.
They twirl and twist in the warm breeze,
Laughing with charm, aiming to please.

With colors that jump and sparkle like glee,
Nature's humor is plain to see.
Each bloom with a joke and a grin,
Tells a story where laughs begin.

Chronicles of the Cultivated

In neat rows where cucumbers hide,
Radishes wear a cap with pride.
Tomatoes blushing in the sun,
Muttering 'We're the chosen one!'

Carrots boast of roots so deep,
While peppers have the best of sleep.
Onions cry from tales of woe,
As zucchini joins the show with glow.

Herbs whisper secrets in the air,
Basil brags of its fragrant flair.
Thyme gets punny, what a prank,
While parsley cheers with a happy clank.

In this garden, there's quite a craze,
Where veggies and herbs cavort and blaze.
With laughter mixed in every bloom,
They chase away the moody gloom.

Sojourn in the Sultry Sun

Under the sun, a joyous spree,
Where dragonflies spin fancy glee.
Bees hum tunes of sweet delight,
Turning day from gray to bright.

Sweating plants and petals glare,
Cacti giggle in their lair.
Succulents, once shy and meek,
Now strut with style, oh so chic.

A breeze kicks up the citrus smell,
As lizards play in a sunlit spell.
Frogs croak jokes that sound like puns,
In this haven where laughter runs.

With every bloom, a burst of cheer,
In a world that's filled with glee and beer.
So let's dance under this golden crown,
And twirl with humor all around.

Herbaceous Ballads

Mint tells tales of freshened breath,
While sage recounts its life and death.
Oregano hums a spicy tune,
Sharing secrets under the moon.

Basil twirls in a pesto show,
While chives are sharp, they steal the glow.
Thyme sits back, sipping on tea,
Watching the mayhem with glee.

Fennel flirts with the vibrant beet,
As ginger jokes about their heat.
With each herb a story's laid,
In this patch of laughter, none afraid.

And at the end, they raise a glass,
To moments, flavors, and a bright green grass.
In herby realms where giggles spark,
A chorus sings from dawn till dark.

Echoing through the Ecosystem

In the forest, leaves do chatter,
Squirrels gossip, it's all a matter.
Flowers giggle as bees take flight,
Nature's laughter echoes, oh what a sight!

Butterflies dance in a wobbly line,
Frogs croak jokes, sipping on brine.
One sneezes loud, a great big splash,
While turtles race—oh wait, they're too brash!

Dandelions puff with pride and cheer,
Telling rumors to those who hear.
A squirrel in shades, he struts with flair,
Claiming the title of 'Nature's Care!'

Amidst the giggles, a raccoon plays,
Stealing cupcakes on sunny days.
So if you wander, do catch the show—
Nature's fun, it's quite the glow!

The Allure of Anarchy in Bloom

Roses wear spiky crowns, feeling grand,
Tulips conspire, plotting on land.
Petals droop, pretending to pout,
While the daisies giggle, oh what a rout!

The wayward weeds march to their own beat,
Shaking their roots, they rave on the street.
"Who needs a gardener?" they sing with glee,
"We're the rebels, come join our spree!"

A sunflower yawns, stretching its stem,
"Chaos in bloom? That's my favorite gem!"
With roots intertwined in a wild dance,
Anarchy thrives, given half a chance.

Bumblebees buzz, with mischief in tow,
Painting the scenery, giving a show.
In this vibrant chaos, life finds a way,
Flower power rules, it's a wacky play!

Chronicles of Color and Chaos

In gardens where colors clash and play,
Petunias argue, come what may.
"Red is best!" says the bold marigold,
While violets giggle at the colors so bold.

Among the chaos, weeds weave a tale,
With clovers sneaking, getting off the trail.
"Oh look, a path from here to there!"
They scamper away, without a care.

A lily rolls its eyes at the fuss,
"Why can't we all just blend like us?"
But the tulips trumpet, standing proud,
In this colorful chaos, they roar aloud.

In this patchwork of laughter and light,
Nature throws parties every night.
So between the tussles, life does enthrall,
In this carnival of colors, we have a ball!

The Heartbeat of Untamed Earth

Among the weeds, a dance of glee,
A dandelion waves, 'Look at me!'
In gardens grand, they strut in flair,
While tulips pout, caught unaware.

Bees buzzing like they own the place,
Grumpy ants in a tiny race.
The soil giggles as roots entwine,
Nature's party, all in rhyme.

Sunlight splashes, paintbrush bright,
Grass tickles toes, oh what a sight!
Frogs croak jokes from lily pads,
Nature's jesters, and it's a lad's!

So grab a seat, enjoy the show,
The quirky blooms put on a glow.
In every petal, laughter bursts,
The untamed earth, our wildest thirst.

The Wild Beneath Our Feet

Roots entwined in a tangled mess,
Nature's ballet, can't help but guess.
A squirrel's slip, oh what a sight!
He blames the acorn, puts up a fight.

Lush grass giggles as we tread on,
With every step, a squishy yawn.
The daisies whisper jokes to bees,
Like nature's punsters, with such ease.

A ladybug winks, as if to say,
'Today's the day we come out to play!'
While petals rain, confetti flare,
The ground's a stage, with laughs to share.

So dance around, make your own beat,
In the nature's circus, beneath our feet.
With every tumble, joy will sprout,
In hidden giggles, there's no doubt!

Petals in the Breeze

Petals flutter, like they're in a race,
Dancing around with silly grace.
A sunflower rolls its big ol' eyes,
Cheering for friends, under sunny skies.

Clouds throw shade in a teasing game,
While poppies giggle, whispering names.
A bumblebee crashes, but what a cheer!
'Keep it up, buddy, no need for fear!'

The wind tells secrets that tickle the trees,
Lost socks sing songs, they're carried with ease.
Sticky honey drips from the hive,
Nature's sweet mess where all thrive.

So grab a bloom, give a spin,
With each petal's giggle, let fun begin.
In this garden wild, joy flows free,
As petals in the breeze laugh with glee.

Meadow's Melody: A Stanza of Nature

In the meadow, daisies dance,
While butterflies take a chance.
Giggling bees buzz all around,
Making music from the ground.

Sunshine winks between the leaves,
A squirrel plots, oh how he grieves.
He drops his acorn, what a scene,
It bounces high, oh what a queen!

The grass tickles every toe,
As we laugh and let it grow.
Nature's jester with a grin,
Invites us all to join the spin.

Every petal wears a smile,
In this field we roam awhile.
Grab a friend and join the fun,
Under the bright and shining sun.

Reveries on a Bed of Green

Lying flat on quilted grass,
Counting clouds as moments pass.
This one's a bunny, that a hat,
Did you see that? Look at that!

Mushrooms wear their tiny caps,
While ants play tag in grand mishaps.
A ladybug lost her way,
Chasing dreams of yesterday.

The breeze whispers joyful tunes,
Underneath the happy moons.
Giggling petals close their eyes,
As the laughter fills the skies.

Each soft tickle from the ground,
In this joy, we're always found.
Nature's laughter, sweet and bold,
In these tales, our hearts take hold.

The Tickle of Grass Beneath Our Toes

Dancing feet on blades so green,
Oh, the funny things we've seen.
The grass, it wiggles, what a tease,
We laugh out loud, oh look at these!

A worm peeks out, says hello,
With a hat made out of snow.
He slides on by, a slippery slick,
Nature's pranks, oh what a trick!

Frogs leap out for ribbit raves,
In their own tiny water graves.
Jumping jests with every splash,
A muddy thrill, oh what a clash!

Underneath the shining sun,
Every moment's filled with fun.
Join the dance, give it a go,
Feel the tickle, let it flow!

Messages Carried by the Wind

Whispers float from leaf to leaf,
A secret shared, beyond belief.
The dandelion seeds take flight,
Spreading giggles through the night.

A breeze with jokes it tries to weave,
Tickling folks who dare believe.
What's that? A joke about a hat?
Oh, only nature could say that!

Clouds parachute, a fluffy fall,
Two squirrels race, who's first to call?
With every gust, a chuckle flies,
Nature's laughter fills the skies.

In this realm of verdant cheer,
Funny tales, all living near.
As the wind sings soft and free,
Join the fun—come laugh with me!

Whispers of Untamed Blooms

In fields where giggles grow so bright,
A sunflower whispers in delight.
Bees are buzzing, busy bees,
While daisies dance with gentle breeze.

Roses snicker, leaning in,
Tulips tease with cheeky grin.
Petals flutter, laughter shared,
Nature's humor, wild and unprepared.

Buttercups play hide and seek,
With bumblebees that wiggle and peek.
Stems are wobbly, trying to stand,
Where flowers joke, it's a funny land.

So join the blooms, let laughter ring,
In this vibrant, floral fling.
From roots to tips, it's all a jest,
In the garden's heart, we're all truly blessed.

Dance of the Meadow Spirits

On a spring day, the breezes flare,
With giggling sprites in the cool fresh air.
They twirl in circles, light as a feather,
Making the flowers laugh all together.

The clovers grin, a cheeky lot,
With jokes about the April spot.
While dandelions puff and blow,
Spreading wishes, making us glow.

Butterflies hitching rides on bees,
Trading tales with giggles and wheeze.
A meadow's stage where bright colors play,
And ticklish petals steal the day.

So come and dance with spirits bold,
In laughter's warmth, let joy unfold.
In meadows where the silly thrive,
Nature's jesters keep the fun alive.

Colors of Nature's Embrace

In splashes bright, the colors clash,
A toddler's painting in a wild splash.
Lemon yellows and bubblegum pink,
Nature's palette makes us wink.

The violets giggle, and poppies cheer,
While frogs croak songs we all can hear.
Lilies pirouette, waving their flair,
While daisies whisper, 'We're quite rare!'

With every shade, a chuckle grows,
Painting meadows in charming flows.
Each hue a joke, a silly tease,
In the field's embrace, we laugh with ease.

So let your spirit run so free,
In this colorful spree, come see.
Nature's canvas, a laughing spree,
Where blossoms bloom with jovial glee.

Beneath the Sunlit Canopy

Under branches, laughter spills,
As squirrels plot their cheeky thrills.
The leaves above are tickled pink,
As sunlight sparkles, wink on wink.

Chipmunks chatter, jokes in tow,
Raccoons join in, stealing the show.
Each rustle shares a secret scheme,
In this shady stage, we all beam.

Butterflies flutter with laughter's grace,
Spreading joy in a fluttering race.
The canopy sings with stories untold,
Of playful tricks, audacious and bold.

So take a seat in nature's play,
Join the fun, come laugh, and stay.
With each giggle beneath the trees,
The world feels lighter, just like a breeze.

Sketches in the Soil's Embrace

In the dirt, I drew a cat,
But ended up with a chubby rat.
Thought I'd sketch a noble tree,
Turns out it's just a shrub, not free.

I tried to paint a sunny sky,
But the clouds came in to say hi.
A worm critiqued my art with glee,
Said, "Buddy, this isn't fit for me!"

When I dug to find some gold,
All I unearthed was pure mold.
And every time I plant a seed,
I end up with a garden of weed.

Oh, the soil laughs at my attempts,
It's a canvas of odd pretense.
In the earth, I find my dreams,
But they're always not what they seem.

The Canvas of Spring's Rapture

Spring's here, I grab my brush,
But the paint always turns to mush.
Tried to color a butterfly,
Instead, it looks like a pie in the sky.

Painted petals, oh so bright,
But they all ended up in a fight.
One pink, one blue, in a spat,
Decided it wanted to be a chat.

The sun jumped in, waving its rays,
Said, "You can't paint me, I'm just here to play!"
So I scribbled clouds like a jester,
Turned out they looked like a big old fester.

Who knew spring could be so wild?
With laughter, mayhem, and madness piled.
Each stroke a giggle, each splash a grin,
Art's a riot, let the fun begin!

Luminescence in Dappled Light

Underneath the trees so grand,
I painted shapes that got out of hand.
What started as a glowing sun,
Turned into a snail on the run.

The shadows laughed, they told me jokes,
As I painted a bunch of croaky frogs.
But each one came out with a beard,
Just one more thing my sketch misunderstood.

The light danced 'round, it tried to play,
But I could not find my way.
A rainbow turned into a slide,
Where birds practiced their silly glide.

Still, I chuckled through the blunders,
As golden beams played like thunder.
In dappled light, where laughter shines,
Art's a crazy blend of whims and lines.

The Ancestral Roots of Color

Roots go down, they swirl and twist,
In colors I never knew existed.
Tried to paint my family tree,
But all I found was a mystery.

Red was grandpa, green was mom,
But what's with uncle—bright purple, like a bomb?
Auntie's color? A sunny yellow blur,
Next, the dog joined in, all splattered fur.

They argue 'bout who's the best of all,
As I step back, I admire the brawl.
Out comes cousin with a wild blue hat,
Sketching a flower that's also a cat!

In hues that scream and colors that clash,
I'm learning that art is also a splash.
Roots intertwine in this color war,
What a family reunion, who could ask for more?

Vignettes from the Wilds

In meadows bright with shades of glee,
A squirrel dances, thinks it's free.
A butterfly joins, in colors bold,
Chasing sunbeams, stories told.

The daffodils gossip, swaying low,
About the bees and their funny glow.
A deer peeks out, with a hint of jest,
While the grass tickles, at nature's best.

Under the sky's expansive dome,
Birds sing tunes that seem like home.
A rabbit munches with quite a flair,
Wreathed in laughter, without a care.

With every breeze, joy's palpable song,
Nature's playground where we all belong.
In these vignettes, life's fun unspools,
A tapestry woven with playful rules.

Petal-Powered Prose

Petals scatter like confetti sweet,
As buzzing bumblebees find their treat.
A ladybug dons her polka-dot dress,
While the daisies chuckle, feeling blessed.

The breeze whispers jokes to the tall, bright grass,
As ants march on, with a sassy sass.
"Did you hear about the flower display?"
"It bloomed so hard, it nearly lost its sway!"

Hummingbirds dart with a sippy sip,
Over petals, they do the ultimate flip.
"Why did the flower shake its stem?"
"To show the world, it's a big gem!"

Between bright blooms, laughter can thrive,
In this garden where whimsies jive.
In petal-powered prose, we find delight,
With silly tales that dance in light.

Wandering Through Wonder

Wandering woods where giggles roam,
A fox with socks claims this as home.
A tree with eyes winks in the sun,
"Tell me a tale, let's have some fun!"

The ferns gossip as fairies pass by,
Spelling secrets to the curious sky.
"Why do snails carry such heavy shells?"
"Because storybooks live where adventure dwells!"

A brook bubbles up with a quirk and splash,
"Why did the fish make such a dash?"
"I heard there's a party, bright and grand,
With snacks made of algae, all hand-planned!"

Wandering through where wonders align,
Nature's laughter, it feels divine.
With each stride taken, joy's revealed,
In this wild world, our dreams are sealed.

The Unfolding of Unseen Stories

In corners where sunlight trickles through,
Unseen tales of nature brew.
A toad croaks jokes by a splashy pond,
Creating ripples, of a world beyond.

The sunflowers stretch, taking their bow,
"Why so tall?" "Just showing how!"
An elder tree laughs at its grey,
"Wisdom's funny, come laugh and play!"

As night unfolds, crickets start to cheer,
With musical notes that tickle the ear.
"Ever heard a pebble dream big?"
"I once knew one that danced a jig!"

The unseen stories tucked away tight,
Burst forth in joy, and share their light.
In the forest's embrace, we find our place,
As laughter blooms in nature's face.

Canvas of the Curved Path

On winding roads where daisies dance,
A squirrel plots a daring prance.
Bumblebees in bow ties zoom,
While ants prepare a dinner room.

A ladybug wears tiny shades,
In this quirky land, no one fades.
Grasshoppers leap with perfect flair,
The earthworms giggle without a care.

Sunflowers cheer as clouds parade,
While butterflies join the grand charade.
A rainbow's smile shades all with glee,
Nature's canvas, wild and free!

Each twist and turn ignites delight,
In nature's joke, we find the light.
The trees all whisper silly rhymes,
As laughter rings through sunny climes.

The Riddle of the Ruins

In ruins old where secrets sleep,
A raccoon swears he'll take the leap.
With ancient stones as his stage props,
He tells a tale that never stops.

The owls hoot wisdom, oh so grand,
While shadows stretch at their command.
A fox runs off with a hat so neat,
Leaving laughter echo in the heat.

Cobwebs flutter like they know,
The postcards of a long-lost show.
Each crumbling brick has quirks to share,
In this puzzling place full of flair.

The stones all chuckle at the past,
"What's lost is found, it's always a blast!"
Join the chorus of the wise and sly,
In these ruins where the jokes never die.

Wild Dreams Through Nature's Eyes

Through nature's lens, what sights we see,
A raccoon in pajamas sipping tea.
A rabbit dreams of moonlit skies,
Plotting to win the big pie prize.

The trees, they giggle at a joke,
While dandelions puff out smoke.
From mushrooms wearing tiny hats,
To chipmunks dancing with the bats.

In this realm where dreams take flight,
A snail races the stars at night.
With a wink and a world of fun,
Nature whispers, "Here, you've just begun!"

Adventures hide in every nook,
Join the laughter in this funny book.
For in these depths of leafy sighs,
Life's a riddle wrapped in surprise!

Garden of the Unsung

In a garden where the shadows play,
The weeds hold court in a quirky way.
With petals talking about the day,
And worms debating on what to say.

The sunflowers gossip, tall and wise,
As drifting leaves wear clever ties.
A hedgehog jests, "I'm quite the catch!"
In this lush maze, nobody's a match.

The carrots dance to a hidden tune,
While ants assemble at high noon.
A daisy dreams in polka dots,
Crafting tales from garden plots.

Each whisper blooms in laughter's scent,
In this garden where time is spent.
Join the fun, don't be so glum,
For every seed holds a punchline's hum.

Hues of the Heartland

In fields of grass, where daisies dance,
The sun's sweet rays give blooms a chance.
A poppy pops its head up high,
While lazy bees just buzz on by.

With strokes of yellow, pink, and blue,
They paint the land, a vibrant view.
A quirky flower, wearing a hat,
Says, "Take a picture! Imagine that!"

The tulip sneezes, petals shake,
The wind plays tricks, they bend and quake.
A daffodil, with cheesy grin,
Says laughter's where our fun begins!

So gather round, enjoy the scene,
In sunlit fields, we laugh and glean.
A patchwork quilt of color bright,
In the heartland's grace, pure delight!

Journal of the Jaunty Jasmine

Oh, Jasmine, with a cheeky flair,
You giggle sweetly in the air.
Your petals gleam, a shiny crew,
With bees that spin like they're in a zoo.

In sunshine's warmth, you sway and sway,
While critters laugh and roam all day.
You tell your tales with breezy spin,
Of all the blunders and cheeky wins.

Your vines climb high, they reach for luck,
While slothful roots still share their muck.
A garden party, where you sing,
In floral hats, the joy you bring!

So pen the notes in fragrant prose,
Where every moment wiggles, grows.
With whiskers twitching and curls so frayed,
Your jaunt is laughter, well portrayed!

Soliloquy of Stems and Stalks

Oh stems and stalks, you stand so tall,
In gentle sway, you jest and sprawl.
With whispers lost in rustling air,
Each leaf a giggle, none a care.

A sunflower cracks a silly grin,
While talking tulips toss a spin.
They banter back, with playful puns,
In nature's theater, there's lots of fun!

A mock debate o'er who's the best,
Which bloom will shine and out the rest?
The daisies boast, but find their fate,
In a windstorm dance, they'll learn to wait.

So gather 'round, the stage is set,
For conversations, you won't forget.
In vibrant colors, they share their tricks,
With sticks that giggle and plants that mix!

Oasis of Color

In a garden bright, where laughter grows,
A rainbow splashes, where nobody knows.
The roses tease the violets rare,
While zinnias giggle without a care.

A cactus wears a flower crown,
While marigolds twirl in a bright gown.
"Oh, what a sight!" the lark will cry,
As petals shimmer beneath the sky.

With every hue, a joke is spun,
And every bloom believes it's fun.
A hibiscus winks, "Come join the spree!"
In this oasis, wild and free!

So let us dance with colors bold,
And share our laughter, bright and gold.
In petals soft and stems that cheer,
We cultivate joy, year after year!

Whispers of the Meadow

In the meadow, grasshoppers leap,
Sharing secrets they struggle to keep.
A butterfly winks, with a flirtatious dance,
While daisies giggle, saying, "Take a chance!"

A squirrel yells, "Where's my acorn stash?"
As ants march around, feeling quite brash.
The sun tickles petals with a warm glow,
Nature's a party, come join the show!

Birds chirp jokes in their high-flying crew,
While flowers blush in colors so new.
Laughter rings out from all around,
In this green comedy, joy can be found!

So kick off your shoes, let your worries cease,
Join the wild fun, embrace nature's peace.
In every rustle, a giggle's in play,
Whispers of joy in the sun-drenched day!

Colors of the Untamed

In a world where the flowers wear crowns,
Pink, yellow, and blue—no sign of frowns.
They strut their stuff, waving in the breeze,
Making the butterflies weak in the knees.

The bees zigzag, like they've lost their way,
Buzzing their tunes, trying hard to play.
"I jive to the nectar! Dance with me now!"
But the flowers just giggle, saying, "Oh wow!"

A daffodil poofs, with a haughty flair,
"Look at me brightening up everywhere!"
While tulips turn heads, shout, "We're quite divine!"
In this riot of colors, laughter does shine!

So let's paint the wild, mix all the hues,
With a brush of the wind, and songs of the blues.
Every mismatched petal tells tales of delight,
In this vibrant playground from morning to night!

Secrets Beneath the Canopy

Under the trees, a turtle's slow tale,
Where squirrels debate if nuts should prevail.
A raccoon sneaks snacks, whispers abound,
As shadows play hide and seek on the ground.

Mushrooms giggle, "We're fun guys, you see!"
Turning the forest into a wild spree.
Leaves rustle softly, sharing sweet gossip,
While hidden foxes plot a comic flip.

A wise old owl hoots, "What's the punchline?"
As tiny frogs jump, saying, "We're just fine!"
The canopy sways with stories galore,
Where laughter and nature always explore.

So come take a peek, at life up above,
Where the trees throw a party, and all of us love.
In this green circus, with secrets to share,
Find joy in the whispers, in the fresh air!

Nature's Ink and Canvas

With twigs as the brushes, and dew as the paint,
The forest creates, with whimsy and quaint.
A cheeky raccoon, with style so bold,
Ponders the canvas, challenging the old.

"Let's splash some berries, and add a dash of fun!"
Said a sprightly fox, "Watch how it's done!"
Wildflowers giggled, "Oh, what a scene!
Nature's an artist; see how we gleam!"

The sky's a swirl, a magnificent hue,
Clouds drift along, they're part of the crew.
A butterfly flits, taking flight with grace,
Leading this folly, in nature's embrace.

So join in the madness, with a brush in your hand,
Create your own joy, let your spirit expand.
In this outdoor gallery, laughter's the theme,
Nature's amusement, a colorful dream!

Epic of the Open Fields

In fields so wide, I trip and fall,
While dandelions laugh and call.
The sun-drenched grass gives way to dance,
I stumble here, but take the chance.

Bees in bow ties, buzzing askew,
Chasing a bloom, all sticky with dew.
One drunk on nectar, flies like a kite,
Aerial antics, oh what a sight!

A rabbit hops in a silly jig,
While squirrels debate a nut so big.
I write it down, what fun we share,
In nature's theater, all laid bare.

So join the frolic, bring your cheer,
No whisper of worries, just laughter here.
In open fields where wild things grow,
Life's comedy blossoms, let's put on a show.

Clusters of Curiosity

There's a patch of weeds, oh what a find,
A home to critters, one of a kind.
What's that noise? A chubby frog,
In search of snacks, or stuck in a bog?

Beetles wear hats, so tight on their heads,
While ants march in rows, like they're well-fed.
What's on the menu? Never quite clear,
But surely there's something, they work without fear.

Butterflies gossip, flitting about,
'Did you hear the news?' they twirl and shout.
I take a note, what a curious lot,
All in their world, while I'm a mere dot.

You'll never know if you don't take a peek,
Nature's the stage, where oddities speak.
In clusters of life, the laughter rings bright,
Join in the fun, from morning till night.

Refrains of the Rising Buds

With each new dawn, the buds do tease,
Stretching their arms, in the warm, soft breeze.
"I can bloom first!" a tulip declares,
While a shy daisy just stares and glares.

A poppy pipes up, full of good cheer,
"Let's start a band, we'll make music here!"
The bees take the stage, hive minds in sync,
Creating a buzz, before we can think.

A daffodil trills, "What's the next song?"
While roses roll their eyes, "That's way too long!"
Laughter erupts, petals gently sway,
Nature's symphony brightens the day.

In gardens alive with a chorus of cheer,
The prints of nature's humor are clear.
Come join the refrain, let your spirit rise,
In blossoms of joy, where laughter applies.

Heartbeats in the Herb Garden

A minty sprig whispers secrets so bold,
While basil tells tales, both funny and old.
Thyme licks a leaf, with a sly little wink,
As dill shares a giggle, over some ink.

Rosemary's bound to a fragrant affair,
With lavender teasing, the perfect bouquet.
"Oh darling," it sighs, "these scents hold the truth,"
While cilantro dreams of its youth as a sleuth.

There's chatter and chuckles, each leaf in a chat,
All herbs have a notion, that's where it's at.
In this herb garden, where humor runs free,
Nature's lush jokes fill the air with glee.

So slice up the fun, with a dash of delight,
Adding some laughter, spice up your night.
With heartbeats of green, let joy take a stand,
In this booming garden, let happiness expand.

Poetic Pollen

In the garden where bees buzz low,
Petals dance with a bright, bold glow.
A daisy winks, a tulip grins,
While shy violets hide their chins.

Sunflowers spin like whirling tops,
Telling tales that never stop.
A bumblebee's a poet, see?
With rhymes sweet as the honey spree!

Dandelions puff with pride,
Making wishes that float and glide.
A group of buds join in the fun,
Sipping dew beneath the sun.

In this floral world of glee,
Petals giggle beneath the tree.
The laughter spreads, it's quite a scene,
As bees and blooms share dreams serene.

Dialogues with the Dandelions

Dandelion, oh wise old sage,
You jest and laugh, your golden page.
Tell me tales of windy nights,
When you danced with stars so bright.

"I've seen the bumblebees in flight,
And squirrels hoarding nuts with might.
A sneeze from me can bring delight,
A puff of joy into the night!"

"Is it true you're just weeds?" I ask,
"Or under blooms you wear a mask?"
"Oh dear, the weeds are but a name,
In gardens, we play a noble game!"

So gather 'round, the flowers say,
Join the fun, let's cheer today!
For every petal knows the score,
In gardens, laughter grows galore!

Fragments of Floral Freedom

Petals play on the summer breeze,
Giggling softly among the trees.
A bloom in pink spots a bee,
"Don't sting me, friend, let's sing with glee!"

Fringed edges of lavender sways,
Whispering secrets of sunny days.
While marigolds stretch on tiptoes,
Peeking under where the soft wind blows.

A dainty bud, it takes a leap,
Rolling down a hill, oh so deep!
"Watch me tumble, watch me spin,
Caution, friends, here comes a grin!"

Freedom blooms with colors bright,
As daisies sway with pure delight.
Join the frolic, don't be shy,
In this garden, laughter's nigh!

Tales from the Thicket

In the thicket where shadows play,
Bramble bushes share their sway.
A rose shouts out, "What's the fuss?"
"Bumblebees need a bus, not us!"

Tulips gossip about the rain,
As violets dance, ignoring the pain.
"Oh dear tulips, let's not pout,
Just spread your petals, let's scream and shout!"

A hedgehog stumbles on a thorn,
I giggle 'cause he looks more worn.
"Dear friends, let us stick together,
Through every storm, in any weather!"

The lilies join in, waving high,
With hope that blooms beneath the sky.
In the thicket, joy takes flight,
On a canvas painted just right!

The Timekeeper's Garden

In the clock's embrace, blooms a daisy,
Ticking and tocking, never too crazy.
A sunflower winks in the afternoon light,
While a cactus grins at the mailman in fright.

The tulips gossip, their secrets in bloom,
Chatting about frogs that give off a fume.
The roses conspire in soft, velvety hues,
Planning a party with mischievous ruse.

A gnome in the corner, hat tilted askew,
Counts every petal, says, "I told you, it's two!"
But daisies just laugh, they don't take a side,
Swinging on breezes, with joyful pride.

As the sun bids adieu, and day takes a bow,
The moon sprinkles stardust, "Hey, I'm back now!"
So dance to the rhythm of nature's own tune,
In the timekeeper's garden, where laughter's a boon.

Enigmas of the Verdant Vale

Down in the vale where the greens all confuse,
A mushroom debates with a snail on the blues.
"Why are you slow?" asks the bright lily bold,
"Because life's a race, and I'm just taking hold!"

The stream chuckles softly, it tumbles with flair,
While the moss-covered rocks pretend not to care.
A raccoon in shadows is flipping through stones,
"Where do I hide my collection of phones?"

The breeze whirls and twirls, scattering leaves,
As squirrels plan heists with acorns, not thieves.
A hedgehog breaks in, "I'm here for the show!"
With quills set ablaze, in the gloaming's soft glow.

In the vale, where enigmas frolic and play,
Each creature is quirky, in a witty display.
As evening descends, all the riddles align,
In the heart of this valley, where jokes intertwine.

Portraits of a Windswept Field

In a field full of daisies, a painting takes flight,
With colors that giggle and dance in the light.
An artist, bemused, slaps paint on his toes,
"Who ordered this chaos?" he laughs as it grows.

The wind adds its brushstrokes, a wild sweeping hand,
Creating a canvas both funny and grand.
A toad hops by, wearing a crown made of grass,
"Is this modern art, or did I just pass?"

The oaks stand tall, lending shade to the spree,
While the thistles sneak up for a selfie, with glee.
A scarecrow yawns, arms draped like a cape,
"Art's like a joke, it's just fine-tuned shape!"

So gather your colors, let laughter persist,
In this portrait of fields, where joy can't be missed.
Each stroke tells a story, all funny and bright,
In the windswept expanse, of pure delight.

Fables Written in Sun and Shadow

In the light, a tortoise writes tales by the lake,
While shadows of snails craft legends to bake.
A parrot squawks out, "What's that tale on your page?"
"A fable of wisdom, and how to act sage!"

The sun tickles leaves, they giggle and sway,
While shadows beneath whisper secrets at play.
A fox with a smirk, spinning yarns of bold quests,
"Do you think they believe all these wild little jest?"

The hare jumps in, "Life isn't always a chase,
Sometimes it's a fable, a laugh in the race."
With jokes woven neatly through sunbeams that gleam,
The world spins a tale more wondrous than dream.

As dusk paints the sky, merging shades of delight,
The fables keep rolling on, long into night.
Each tale a reminder, a wink from the day,
That life's the best story, in every wild way.

Serenade of the Sunlit Fields

Beneath the sky so bright and blue,
The flowers giggle, all in view.
Bees buzz like they own the place,
While butterflies flaunt their silly grace.

Each blossom wears a silly hat,
A poppy dressed as a chubby cat.
They trade jokes and share a laugh,
In this field, there's no math!

The wind joins in with a playful twist,
Tickling petals, a breezy mist.
Dandelion seeds float like spies,
Planning pranks in the sunny skies.

So come and dance on this merry ground,
Where laughter echoes all around.
In fields so bright, the fun won't cease,
Here, every petal's a burst of peace.

The Dance of the Daisies

The daisies gather, a ragtag crew,
With floppy hats and a wild view.
They twist and turn, with every glance,
Inviting all to join their dance.

One daisy's tripped over a bee,
Saying, "Hey, watch where you fly near me!"
Others chuckle, bending low
At this less-than-graceful show.

They form a circle, arms linked tight,
Spinning around in pure delight.
With every spin, they drop their shoes,
Giving the grass its chance to snooze.

The sun beams bright, a gleeful light,
While daisies dance from day till night.
In this garden of laughter and cheer,
They bloom with joy, year after year.

Inked in Wild Elegance

On parchment leaves, the ink does flow,
With tales of plants that steal the show.
Each petal writes its own sweet verse,
In a world that's slightly perverse.

The lilies sigh, with a dramatic flair,
"We're the queens, not a single care!"
While roses roll their beauty eyes,
Scandalous gossip under the skies.

Sunflowers chuckle at the shade,
"Don't worry, we've got it made!"
They stretch their necks with utmost pride,
Unbothered by gossip far and wide.

And in this garden, the laughter grows,
Each bloom a story, as everyone knows.
With ink and petals, the pages bend,
In this book of life, the fun won't end.

Verses from the Verdant

In a realm where green reigns supreme,
The shrubs whisper secrets, plot and scheme.
Thistles wear crowns of pointy pride,
While ferns huddle close, shy but dignified.

The peonies prance in a floral parade,
Mocking the clovers—"You're just a shade!"
But clovers wink, with a giggly cheer,
"Luck's on our side, so have no fear!"

The violets giggle, in hues of blue,
While waving their leaves, saying, "Look, it's true!"
They conjure up laughter with every bloom,
Filling the air with fragrant perfume.

So join the verses from this lush land,
With flowers and laughter hand in hand.
In every leaf, there's humor to find,
In the verdant realms, joy's intertwined.

Strokes of Flora's Brush

In the garden, six bees conspire,
With nectar dreams, they dance and tire.
Petal battles, a colorful fray,
Humming with laughter, all through the day.

Lilly spills secrets on how to sway,
While daisies giggle in a sunlit play.
A wild rose winks, with a thorny jest,
Claiming the title of floral best.

Violets gossip beneath leafy hats,
Whispering tales of snooty brats.
In this patch, silliness reigns supreme,
Nature's own stand-up, living the dream.

So here's to the blooms with cheeky grins,
Sprouting joy, oh, where to begin?
Each leafy laugh, a colorful show,
In this happy garden, humor will grow.

Chronicles of the Untamed Terrain

Under skies where the freest winds blow,
Mossy rocks witness tales of woe.
A tumbleweed rolls, with sass and spin,
Plotting its path, ready to begin.

Ants in a line, like a circus parade,
Confetti crumbs shift, making their trade.
Grassy knolls chuckle at the drill,
As flowers wink, what's with the thrill?

A fox takes a nap, what a sight to see,
Dreaming of rabbits, or maybe just me!
The earth ticks along with a playful chime,
In this wild realm, there's never a crime.

Join the fun, let your spirit fly,
In this terrain, you never know why.
With petals and tails, and laughter so bright,
Nature's own mischief is pure delight.

A Tapestry of Earth's Voices

In the meadows where the grass does sway,
Each blade a word in the game of play.
Chirping crickets hit the high note,
While wind serenades, with a gentle quote.

Butterflies gossip in bold flight paths,
With polka dot dresses, oh what laughs!
Dandelions puff out whims with glee,
Spreading their fluff like a nature spree.

The brook spills secrets, a bubbly chat,
As frogs leapt over like acrobats.
Every rustle, a chuckle, every breeze,
An orchestra of joy beneath the trees.

So listen close, the earth's humor sings,
From tiny ants to the birds on wings.
A lively tapestry, woven with cheer,
Nature's voice ringing, far and near.

The Cry of the Wayward Seed

A seed takes off on an unplanned ride,
Sailing through puddles and fields wide.
With hopes of blooming, it tumbles and rolls,
Dreaming of sunbeams, in dirt it strolls.

"Weeds are just flowers with stories to tell,"
Said the dandelion, feeling quite swell.
"Don't fret, little seed, for you'll find your spot,
In this wild journey, give it all you've got!"

The wind howled jokes; the clouds burst with laughter,
Each twist and turn a scene from hereafter.
Each sprout a comedy, the dirt a stage,
As roots dig deep, breaking out of the cage.

With every bloom, laughter's seeds are sown,
In nature's theatre, you're never alone.
So dance, little seed, in the wild embrace,
For life is a riot, a flourish of grace!

Portrait of a Breeze

A tickle on the nose, a poke in the hair,
Subtle dances, floating everywhere.
Whispers of mischief through the meadow's sway,
Giggling with flowers, they laugh and play.

A gust twirls the hair of a daisy out wide,
As clovers shake hands with the butterflies' glide.
Sneaky little zephyrs, swirling with glee,
Decorating the sky with a flowery spree.

With every soft push, it sends seeds on a flight,
Providing the pollen for a party tonight.
"Who invited the bees?" a tulip will ask,
But the breeze just giggles, sidestepping the task.

A brush against branches, a rustle of grass,
Nature's own joker, quite ready to pass.
Spreading cheer in the knowing, a mystical tease,
Life's silly conductor, the portrait of breeze.

Nature's Storytellers

A squirrel in spectacle, narrates with flair,
With acorns for props, it performs in midair.
Each skitter and chatter, a tale to unfold,
About brave fern battles and secrets retold.

The birds chirp in chorus, their songs interlace,
Crafting legends of love at a dizzying pace.
Chasing each other, they swoop and they dive,
In this forest theater, they feel so alive!

Beneath the cool canopy, shadows can play,
While mushrooms can giggle at sunlight's delay.
And under a leaf, a snail takes a peek,
"Is that a new story? Oh, do share next week!"

Together they yarn, in the breeze they conspire,
Nature's confessions are mixed with good cheer.
In a world full of whimsy, what fun it must be,
To listen to tales told by creatures so free!

Expressions of the Windswept Field

In the field where the daisies dance cheek to cheek,
And the piquant breeze makes the tall grasses squeak.
The poppies are gossiping, sharing the news,
About how the sun came to hide in its hues.

With laughter that bubbles, the petals unite,
A colorful chorus in the soft golden light.
Tickled by the wind, they twirl in delight,
As butterflies swoon, having dreams take flight.

"Who's that jigging wildly?" a dandelion sighs,
"It's just the spare breeze, wanting to surprise!"
So flowers start tumbling, in whimsical joy,
Creating a dance floor, oh what a ploy!

As evening approaches, the stars start to peep,
Even crickets are chuckling, as they start to leap.
In the windswept field, such gaiety thrives,
Nature's own stage, where the fun never dies!

Views from the Verdant Vantage

Up high on the hill where the whimsy is real,
The grass whispers secrets, its soft, verdant feel.
From daisies to thistles, they gather and scheme,
Plotting surprises like a marvelous dream.

"Did you see that ladybug, such a show-off?"
It twirls in midair, a dazzling scoff.
While raindrops peek through leaves, a ticklish rain play,
Spreading silliness in their own merry way.

The view from above is a riot of cheer,
Where the critters below seem to dance with no fear.
A fox in a bowtie struts in the sun,
And that's just a glimpse; oh, there's more to come!

With clouds as their audience, and sunlight a beam,
The vista erupts in a whimsical dream.
Where nature's expressions twirl without end,
From views up on high, there's always a trend!

Conversations with the Cosmos

I asked the stars for a joke,
They twinkled back, 'We're no smoke!'
The moon just laughed and pointed right,
'At least we shine throughout the night!'

I pondered deep on this advice,
A comet dashed, 'Hey, not so nice!'
Between the planets, laughter flew,
Who knew space had a prank or two?

The sun yelled down, 'Share a pun!'
'Don't make me rise; it's not that fun!'
The black holes snickered with delight,
Swallowing jokes that vanished from sight.

So here's my truth: with stars to chat,
The universe loves a good-natured spat!
In endless space, jokes find their way,
Just keep the laughter—come what may!

Blooming in Solitude

A daisy stood all on her own,
Saying, 'In silence, I've grown!'
The roses giggled, adorned with flair,
'You must be lonely, do you care?'

She replied, 'Oh, trust me, it's grand!
No insects buzzing close at hand.'
The tulips joined with a feathery sigh,
'But can you dance? We must know why!'

'Why dance?' said she, 'I sway with breeze,
When twirling alone, I do it with ease!'
The sunflowers chuckled, 'What a sight!
Blooming in solitude, isn't it bright?'

So if you find a lone flower sprout,
Remember her joy, don't give a shout.
In solitary bliss, she dances so free,
Why not join her, just let it be!

The Lullaby of Lavender

In fields of purple, whispers play,
Lavender sings the night away.
'Close your eyes, let dreams take flight,
I'll wrap you snug until morning light.'

With bees in tune, a funny choir,
'Buzz off, dear friends, our tales inspire!'
The moon blushed pink, a sight so rare,
As flowers shared secrets, dancing in air.

A breeze wove through, a gentle tease,
'Roses are red, but I'm the breeze!'
Lavender giggled, petals aglow,
'Let's keep it light; don't steal my show!'

So when you smell that calming scent,
Remember the laughter, the time well spent.
In fields of laughter, all is well,
With lavender's lullaby weaving its spell.

Reflections in the Rain Garden

Raindrops tap like little feet,
Puddles laugh—a splashy greet.
'What's your secret?' I asked a rose,
'How do you shine when the water flows?'

The rose replied, 'Just let it rain,
I dance in droplets, forget the pain!'
'Let's splash and play, oh what a sight!'
Lilies chimed in, 'Come join the flight!'

A fern swooped down, holding a leaf,
'Let's catch drips, no room for grief!'
Together they twirled, amidst the fun,
In the garden, where laughter spun.

So when the sky decides to cry,
Join the plants, give joy a try.
In reflections of rain, laughter's found,
In a garden where joy knows no bound!

Journeys in Bloom

In the garden of dreams, I tripped on a spade,
Chasing bees with a grin, I made quite the raid.
Petunias were gossiping, daisies took flight,
While I skidded on grass, it was quite the sight.

A dandelion danced, with a laugh all its own,
It whispered sweet secrets, in the softest tone.
I swung wildly on vines, felt like Tarzan in style,
Until a rogue weed tickled, and I fell with a smile.

Butterflies chuckled as I swirled round and round,
With pollen as confetti, I hit the ground.
Roses rolled their eyes, in their thorns they did hide,
While I plotted my escape from this floral wild ride.

Through petals of laughter, my journey unfolds,
With bloom-printed stories, and giggles untold.
Each color a chuckle, each scent a delight,
In this zany garden, everything feels right.

Flora's Footprints

In the meadow of mischief, I found a bright shoe,
A squirrel wore it proudly, with nary a clue.
He twirled with a walnut, as if in parade,
While I laughed at the sight, my worries delayed.

Sunflowers were feasting on rays from the sky,
Telling corny jokes that made butterflies fly.
A thistle wore glasses, looked ready to teach,
While I tried to join in, but it felt out of reach.

With daisies as dancers and clovers in line,
I took off my shoes, said, "Let's twirl and dine!"
But the ground started giggling, a ticklish spree,
As petals ruffled softly, amused by the glee.

When the sun set down, with blush on its face,
The garden held laughter, a magical space.
With footprints in flora, I waved them goodnight,
In dreams, they still dance, 'neath the moon's silver light.

Seasons Scribbled in Color

Spring threw a party, with flowers galore,
Balloons made of blossoms, and bees at the door.
A tulip in a tutu twirled 'neath the sun,
While I tried to keep up, but the fun had begun.

Summer strutted in, wearing shades and a grin,
With sunflowers gossiping, 'Is that really him?'
I tiptoed through daisies, pretending to sway,
But tripped on a twig, what a comical display!

Autumn arrived, with leaves like confetti,
Frolicking squirrels made the scene less steady.
They challenged my balance, I fell with a thud,
Wrapped in a quilt of orange and mud.

Winter then chuckled, in frosty delight,
Made snowmen with hats that looked quite out of sight.
With jingles of laughter, the seasons took flight,
In a scrapbook of colors, they danced through the night.

Verses from the Verdant Floor

In a meadow of jokes, where the grass likes to tease,
A caterpillar giggled, sprawled out on its knees.
It wore such a grin, like it knew some grand lore,
While I couldn't help chuckling, rolling on the floor.

The mushrooms held meetings, their caps in a fuss,
Debating the best shade—in pink, or in rust?
While I pondered my snack, a blueberry affair,
They waved me to join, but I just couldn't dare.

Ferns whispered secrets, intrigued by the winds,
While I tried to decipher their leafy chagrins.
A ladybug party was all the rage,
With tiny disco lights on an acorn stage.

As twilight approached, the garden burst forth,
With laughter and light, giving joy a new worth.
In verses of verdure, adventures took flight,
Each thread of the tale twinkling softly at night.

Secrets of the Rugged Hills

In the hills where bumbles play,
A squirrel stole my snack today.
With nuts and berries held so tight,
He waved goodbye, a comical sight.

The cacti wear a spiky crown,
But scared off the bears from town.
They dance in moonlight, all a-twirl,
Creating chaos, like a whirl.

A hilltop gopher digs a hole,
He thinks he's found the perfect bowl.
With mud and grass, he hosts a feast,
Inviting all, both great and least.

So if you wander up this way,
Beware the squirrels and gopher play.
For secrets hide in every nook,
A laughing rhyme, a storybook.

The Language of Unruly Petals

Petals bouncing in the breeze,
With whispering secrets, oh, such tease.
One stamped their foot, a flower fight,
As bees laughed loudly, feeling right.

Daisies shouted, 'Pick me, me!'
While roses sulked, 'Just let us be!'
The tulips tried to form a band,
Played notes so silly, in the sand.

A dandelion advised with care,
'Blow your dreams into the air!'
But then it sneezed, and oh, what mess,
A cloud of fluff—nature's jest!

So listen close when petals chat,
Their gossip's wild, imagine that!
In every bloom, laughter grows,
A garden filled with silly prose.

Symphony of the Meadow Breeze

The breeze hums tunes of funny tales,
As butterflies wear tiny veils.
A caterpillar doing the jig,
While crickets laugh, doing a big.

The daisies swayed, a line-up dance,
Inviting ants to join their prance.
Collecting pollen, they all found,
A raucous beat upon the ground.

A bumblebee buzzed off key,
Yet sang aloud in harmony.
With grasshoppers clapping all around,
Nature's concert, so profound!

So if you wander in the field,
Listen close to what's revealed.
For in each breeze and silly sound,
A joyful symphony is found.

Echoes in the Garden of Dreams

In the garden where giggles ring,
Each flower wears a playful bling.
The tulips twist and spin with glee,
While gnomes juggle, one, two, three!

A rose decided to tell a joke,
But thorns gave it a little poke.
It blushed so red, the crowd burst in,
Laughter erupted—let the fun begin!

Lavender sneezed and lost her grace,
Fell flat into a daisy's face.
They both stood up in fits of giggles,
As daisies danced and did their wiggles.

So visit the dreams where echoes play,
In the garden, fun's here to stay.
Where each petal has a tale,
Of whimsy, laughter, and a sneak attack of snail.

Whispers Among the Petals

In gardens where the daisies chat,
The tulips giggle, imagine that!
The roses gossip, oh what a sight,
While sunflowers dance in pure delight.

A bee buzzes by, it wears a grin,
Claiming it's the best at pollen kin.
The violets chuckle, hiding their hue,
As they plot a party just for the crew.

Fuzzy caterpillars tell tales so grand,
Of adventures they dream in the leaf-laden land.
"Let's throw a bash," says the cheeky fern,
While greenery giggles, waiting their turn.

Amidst the joy of this floral bazaar,
A lizard sings softly, strumming a guitar.
So come join the laughter, under the sun,
In this quirky garden, where life's just fun!

Leafy Love Letters

Oh sweet little leaf, on the branch you sway,
You whisper dear notes of love every day.
Your fluttering gestures, a romantic tease,
Make the flowers blush in the warm summer breeze.

The petals take notes, writing sonnets in green,
In a world filled with laughter, they're quite the scene.
With hearts made of sunlight and roots in the ground,
They flirt with the shadows where giggles abound.

A rosemary sprig pens a letter with flair,
To a basil so fragrant, with scents in the air.
The lavender winks, oh what a romance,
In the garden's embrace, the flowers all dance.

So grab a leaf, and write your own rhyme,
In this patch of laughter, we're lost in the prime.
With petals and leaves, our love will take flight,
In the lush pages of day turning to night.

In the Arms of Flora

Nestled in flora, I find such surprise,
Where daisies wear crowns and violets rise.
A sunflower hugs me, so warm and so bright,
While the daffodils giggle, what a silly sight!

The poppies are partying, dressed red and bold,
Complaining of bees that won't leave them, I'm told.
With petals a-twirl in the sun's golden glow,
Flora's embrace makes the merriment flow.

From buttercups gleaming to lilacs that sway,
They cheer for the joy found in every new day.
In this whimsical world, where laughter's the aim,
Even thorns wear a smile, they're part of the game!

So let's twirl with the daisies, skip under the sky,
In the arms of this flora, where time just flies by.
With giggles and joy, we'll dance in the light,
In this glorious garden, everything feels right.

The Speak of Spontaneity

In a blink, the petals dance to their tune,
With twirls and spins under the light of the moon.
The daisies shout, "Come join our parade!"
A wild romp begins, no plans to be made!

Butterflies flutter, with laughter they tease,
As ferns whisper secrets in the teasing breeze.
With a hop and a skip, the garden ignites,
In the speak of spontaneity, the joy unites!

The leaves, they conspire, to sprout and to play,
With unplanned antics, making each day.
The mint sips a cocktail of dew and delight,
While the sage tells a tale that stretches the night.

Jump in the fray, feel the fun all around,
In this crazy garden, pure joy can be found.
With laughter erupting, leave worries behind,
In the speak of spontaneity, true bliss is defined!

Tapestry of Flora Dreams

In a garden where daisies plot,
Their bright schemes with a laughing thought,
Roses gossip in perfumed hues,
While sleeping tulips hum their blues.

The daisies dance, twirl around,
While the violets giggle, sound profound,
Lily pads wear hats made of mist,
Where bees come for tea and sweet tryst.

Peonies trade tales of sun and rain,
As dandelions laugh, they're so insane,
Each petal a story, a silly jest,
In this floral realm, we're all guests.

So join the fun, let out a cheer,
For these blooms hold laughter ever near,
A tapestry of colors and charm,
In the garden, nothing's a harm.

Messages on the Wind

Whispers float on soft summer air,
Tulips shout secrets without a care,
Dandelions puff their wishes wide,
While butterflies giggle, they can't hide.

A sunflower shouts, 'Look at me!'
It's fashion week for bees, oh glee!
Hoping to catch the latest craze,
In this floral world, we're in a daze.

The breeze picks up, a playful tune,
As pansies prank in the light of the moon,
Petals join in, they're quite the band,
While crickets tap dance on the land.

So send your letter, make your plea,
With flowers as poets, wild and free,
Messages on the wind take flight,
In this blossom-filled world, pure delight.

When Earth Speaks in Petals

When whispers of petals break the ground,
And earth sets laughter all around,
Iris grins wide, in purple flair,
While tulips chuckle, without a care.

The soil beneath, a stage for jest,
As each bloom tries to outdo the rest,
A daffodil boasts, 'I shine the most!'
While cacti roll eyes and mockingly boast.

Bees wear tiny crowns, feel quite grand,
While roses swap hats, a silly band,
With colors that make the sun jealous,
In this playful scene, all is precious.

So when the petals start to sway,
Listen close to what they say,
For in the laughter of bloom divine,
The earth speaks volumes, bright and fine.

Chronicles of the Enchanted Garden

In the garden of giggles, tales unfold,
Where each bloom's a story, bright and bold,
Lavender lounges with a witty quip,
While marigolds dance, let the laughter rip.

Ferns tickle each other, oh what a sight,
As garden gnomes plot their midnight flight,
They throw a party, under the moon,
With mushrooms all singing a silly tune.

The veggies debate who's the best of all,
While radishes roll and tomatoes fall,
A jester bee buzzes, wearing a crown,
In this enchanted place, jokes never drown.

So come join the frolic, embrace the fun,
For in this garden, joy weighs a ton,
Chronicles spun with laughter and cheer,
In the petals and leaves, the magic is near.

www.ingramcontent.com/pod-product-compliance
Lightning Source LLC
Chambersburg PA
CBHW071853160426
43209CB00003B/543